French Horn Student

by James Ployhar

To the Student

Level III of the Belwin "Student Instrumental Course" is a continuation of Levels I and II of this series or may be used to follow any other good intermediate instruction book. It is designed to help you become an excellent player on your instrument in a most enjoyable manner. It will take a reasonable amount of work and CAREFUL practice on your part. If you do this, learning to play should be a valuable and pleasant experience.

Please see the top of Page 5 for practice suggestions and other comments that should be very helpful.

To the Teacher

Level III of this series is a continuation of the Belwin "Student Instrumental Course", which is the first and only complete course for individual instruction of all band instruments. Like instruments may be taught in classes. Cornets, Trombones, Baritones and Basses may be taught together. The course is designed to give the student a sound musical background and, at the same time, provide for the highest degree of interest and motivation. The entire course is correlated to the band oriented sequence.

Each page of this book is planned as a complete lesson, however, because some students advance more rapidly than others, and because other lesson situations may vary, lesson assignments are left to the discretion of the teacher.

To make the course both authoritative and practical, the books in Level III are co-authored by a national authority on each instrument in collaboration with James Ployhar.

The Belwin "Student Instrumental Course" has three levels: elementary, intermediate and advanced intermediate. Each level consists of a method and two or three supplementary books. Levels II and III each have four separate correlated solos with piano accompaniment. The chart below shows the correlating books available with each part.

The Belwin "STUDENT INSTRUMENTAL COURSE" - A course for individual and class instruction of LIKE instruments, at three levels, for all band instruments.

EACH BOOK IS COMPLETE IN ITSELF BUT ALL BOOKS ARE CORRELATED WITH EACH OTHER

METHOD
"The French Horn Student"
For Individual or Class Instruction.
(cannot be used with other brass instruments.)

ALTHOUGH EACH BOOK CAN BE USED SEPARATELY, IDEALLY, ALL SUPPLEMENTARY BOOKS SHOULD BE USED AS COMPANION BOOKS WITH THE METHOD

STUDIES AND MELODIOUS ETUDES

Supplementary scales, warm-up and technical drills, musicianship studies and melody-like etudes, all carefully correlated with the method.

TUNES FOR TECHNIC

Technical type melodies, variations, and "famous passages" from musical literature for the development of technical dexterity.

FRENCH HORN SOLOS

Four separate correlated solos, with piano accompaniment, written or arranged by James D. Ployhar:

Champagne Song............*Mozart*
March of the Grenadiers..*Ployhar*
Alleluia from "Exsultate,
    Jubilate"......................*Mozart*
Intrepido ....*Ployhar*

Fingering Chart For The Double French Horn (F & Bb)

Since the Double Horn is now in common use the following chart contains fingerings for both the F Horn and the Bb Horn. The use of the Bb Horn allows for greater accuracy in the high register and facilitates tone production in the low register. Not all tones are practical on the Bb Horn, however, because of intonation problems.

Many players prefer to use their Bb Horn when they reach second line G# and continue to use it throughout the upper register.

The Bb Horn is also employed from low F down to low C.

If you have a Double Horn your teacher will advise you when to use it. When playing lip slurring exercises in this book the fingerings indicated are for F Horn.

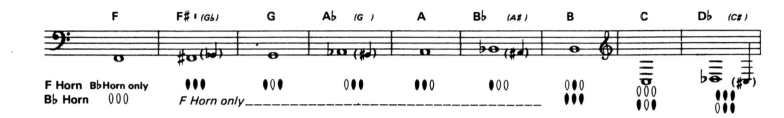

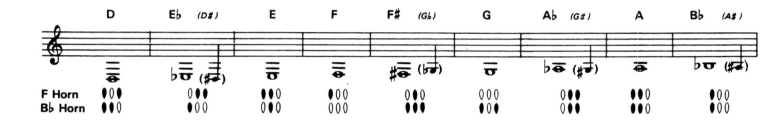

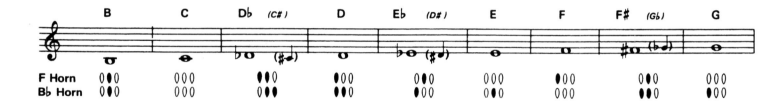

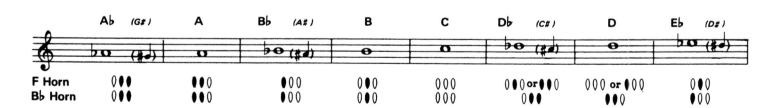

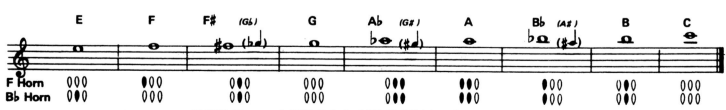

Muting

The sound of the muted horn is created by placing the right hand into the bell so that the bell is all but closed. The fingers are held firmly against the far side of the bell while the palm of the hand is lowered so as to make firm contact with the near side of the bell. As a result the tubing of the horn is actually shortened, and the player will discover that each note will sound one half-tone higher than intended. To compensate, the player must finger every muted note one half-tone lower than written.

The most common sign used to indicate a muted horn is + . However, you may find such terms as *"Con Sordini"*, *"Gestopft"* and *"Bouche"*. An open horn is indicated by the symbol o , or the words *"open"* or *"natural"*.

AS WRITTEN:

Mutes are available for the French Horn in both the transposing and non-transposing variety. The use of the non-transposing mute allows the player to read the notation just as written.

Bass Clef

Most of the music written for the French Horn is written in the treble clef, but occasionally you will find music written in the bass clef. This is done to facilitate the reading of music in the lower register. The following is a descending chromatic scale as it appears in the treble clef and as it would appear in the bass clef:

Transposition

Although the *Horn in E♭* is perhaps the most common transposition problem confronting the French Horn student he may be faced with the task of playing parts written in a number of different keys. The following shows the C scale as it would appear on horn parts written in various keys and as it would be played on the *F Horn*. The new key signature may be envisioned by adding the necessary sharps or flats.

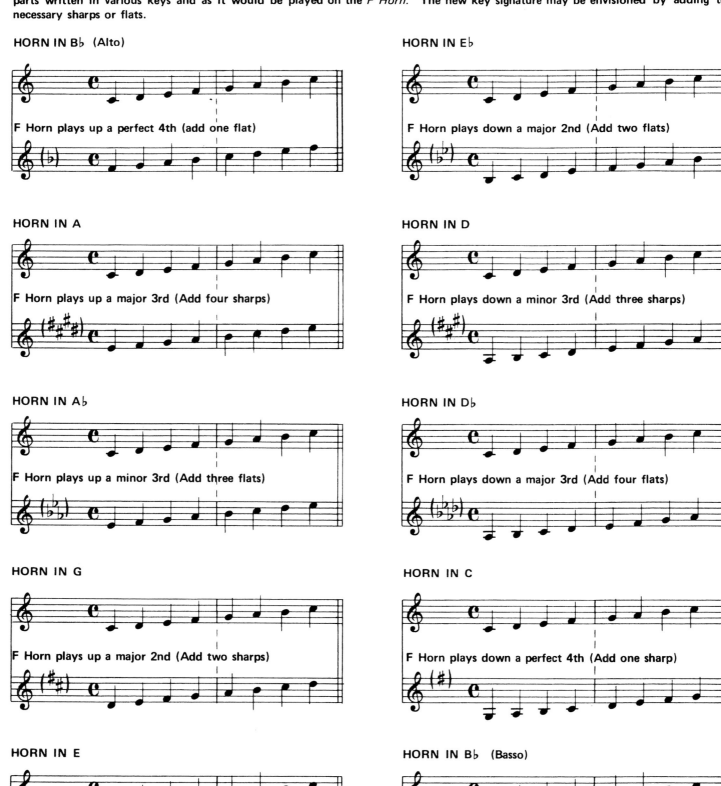

HORN IN B♭ (Alto)

F Horn plays up a perfect 4th (add one flat)

HORN IN E♭

F Horn plays down a major 2nd (Add two flats)

HORN IN A

F Horn plays up a major 3rd (Add four sharps)

HORN IN D

F Horn plays down a minor 3rd (Add three sharps)

HORN IN A♭

F Horn plays up a minor 3rd (Add three flats)

HORN IN D♭

F Horn plays down a major 3rd (Add four flats)

HORN IN G

F Horn plays up a major 2nd (Add two sharps)

HORN IN C

F Horn plays down a perfect 4th (Add one sharp)

HORN IN E

F Horn play down a minor 2nd (Add five sharps)

HORN IN B♭ (Basso)

F Horn plays down a perfect 5th (Add one flat)

A Few Important Practice Suggestions:

1. Set a regular practice time and make every effort to practice at this time.

2. ALWAYS practice carefully. Careless practice is a waste of time. Learn to play each line exactly as written. Later there may be times when certain freedoms may be taken.

3. The instrument must always be clean and in good playing condition.

4. The development of careful and accurate playing habits is essential if you are to become a good player. Proper hand, finger, mouth or embouchure and body position is absolutely necessary for best results. Always keep relaxed.

5. COUNT AT ALL TIMES.

Daily Warm-Up Studies:

The lines below are intended for use as daily warm-up drill, embouchure or lip-building studies, and for the development of technical proficiency. They should be used as an addition or supplement to the regular lesson assignment. Use certain lines as a routine with changes from time to time as suggested by your teacher.

6

Please see the book "Tunes for French Horn Technic" for more melodies that provide for further technical development.

Please see the book STUDIES AND MELODIOUS ETUDES, Level III (Advanced Intermediate) for more scale and technical studies that correlate with Method Book III.

a minor (Harmonic Form)   Arpeggios

a minor (Melodic Form)   Arpeggios

Etude In A Minor

Allegro

Chromatic Study

Also, tongue every note.

A STUDY IN PHRASING   Gypsy Melody   SARASATE
Slowly and dramatically

The Wild Horseman

SCHUMANN

Allegro

Fine

D. C. al Fine

8

INTERVALS

Practise slowly, and then try for speed.

Articulation Etude

KOPPRASCH

ALSO PLAY:

Compare measures 1 and 3. Play all rhythms accurately.

Rhythm Etude

Celebrated Waltz

BRAHMS

*See page 39.

LIP SLURS

Scale Study In F Major

Interval Study

Syncopation Study

Articulation Etude

① d minor (Harmonic Form) — Arpeggios

② d minor (Melodic Form) — Arpeggios

Etude In D Minor

③ Allegretto — *mf*

Chromatic Scale

④

Also, tongue every note.

Keep triplets and eighth notes even.

⑤

Also play a Major 2nd lower.

Garry Owen
(Interval And Transposition Study)

(Horn in E♭
Lively)

⑥

1   2

INTERVALS

Practice slowly, and then try for speed.

Articulation Etude

Practice slowly, and then try for speed!

Waltz Melody

A TONE AND PHRASING STUDY

BRAHMS

ACCURACY STUDY

Slowly

Repeat using various dynamic levels: $pp - p - mp - mf - f - ff$

Etude

ARBAN

Moderato

Lip Slurs

1st + 3rd Valves_____   2nd + 3rd Valves_____   1st + 2nd Valves_____

1st Valve_____   2nd Valve_____   open_____

Scale Study In G

Syncopation Study

In Two

TONGUING EXERCISE
Work for speed!

Theme From "Light Cavalry Overture"

von SUPPE

Allegro

e minor (harmonic form)

Arpeggios

1

e minor (melodic form)

Arpeggios

2

E Minor Scale Study

3

STUDY IN DYNAMICS

Slowly

4

1st. time **pp p-mp-mf-f-ff** ——— *simile*

2nd. time **ff-f-mf-mp-p-pp** ———

Rhythm Etude

Moderato

(♪ = ♪)

5

(♪ = ♪)

Berceuse From "Jocelyn"

Strive to play this melody in a musically artistic manner. Don't approach it in a strict, mechanical way. Work for good tone, proper phrasing and stylistic expression. Consider the impression you are making on the listener.

GODARD

Andantino

6

p

cresc.   *f*   *rall.*

a tempo

pp

p   *f*   *pp*

*See page 21

14

INTERVALS

Practice slowly, and then try for speed.

Articulation Study

SCHANTL

ABBREVIATIONS

Comparing ⁶⁄₈ And ¹²⁄₈

Andante Cantabile

P. I. TSCHAIKOWSKY

OCTAVE SLURS

Scale Study In Bb

CHROMATIC SCALE (LOW REGISTER)

Also, tongue each note.

Interval Study

Work for speed with accuracy!

ACCURACY STUDY

Slowly

Repeat using various dynamic levels.

Waltz From "Serenade For Strings"

TSCHAIKOWSKY

*See page 39.

1 g minor (harmonic form)   Arpeggios

2 g minor (melodic form)   Arpeggios

Etude In G Minor

3 Allegro moderato
mf

Study In Syncopation

4
Count: 1 + 2 + 3 +   1 + 2 + 3 +

Sailors' Hornpipe

This melody encompasses the most practical range of the French Horn. Try to perfect it, and strive to play all of the intervals accurately. Observe articulation markings.

5 Moderato
mf

Intervals

Maintain evenly divided eighth notes and triplets.

Articulation Etude

Allegro vivace

Chromatic Scale

Also, slur each measure.

Czech Dance

SMETANA

Moderato

poco cresc.

* See page 39.

LIP SLURS

Scale Study In D

Staccato Study

Articulation Etude

*See page 22.

1 b minor (harmonic form) — Arpeggios

2 b minor (melodic form) — Arpeggios

A Tonguing Study

MICHIELS

Allegretto

Triplet Etude

Allegro moderato

Serenade

SCHUBERT

Slowly — In a songlike style. When necessary, tongue in a soft, legato manner.

rit.

20

INTERVALS

Practice slowly, and then try for speed.

simile

Articulation Etude

Moderato

mf

Solvejg's Song

EDVARD GRIEG

A PHRASING STUDY

Andante

p

f

p

a tempo

poco rit.

mf

p

LOW REGISTER STUDY
Work for speed!

simile

Etude

SCHANTL

Allegretto

p

p

Fine

p

mf

f

p

f

p

D. C. al Fine

OCTAVE SLURS

Slowly

Tonguing Exercise

Tongue cleanly.   Work for speed.

Articulation Etude

Moderato

Since a dot placed after a note adds one-half of its value, two dots placed after a note will add one-half *plus* one-quarter of its value.

As written:

As played:

March Pontificale

C. GOUNOD

Allegro

Lip Slurs

Slowly

Scale Study In Eb Major

1st + 3rd Valves

Three evenly divided sixteenth notes (triplets) may be played in place of an eighth note:

Allegro animato (Fast and lively)

KLING

Etude

Lively

c minor (harmonic form) — Arpeggios

c minor (melodic form) — Arpeggios

Etude In C Minor

Allegretto

ACCURACY STUDY

Slowly

Rhythm Etude

Allegro

Count: 1 2

March Melody

F. SCHUBERT

Also play a Major 2nd lower (Horn in Eb)

Intervals

Articulation Study

SCHANTL

Moderato

Rhythm Etude

Watch for changes in the time signature!

Theme From Symphony No. 6

TSCHAIKOWSKY

Andante (with much expression)

A Major Scale   Arpeggios

Scale Study In A Major

simile

Rhythm Etude

Allegro con brio (Fast and with spirit)

A TONGUING TUNE

Work for speed!

Landler

This melody will help you develop your ability to hear intervals of 3rds, 4ths, 5ths and 6ths. Listen carefully as you play, and be sure each interval is accurate.

SCHUBERT

Allegretto

1 f♯ minor (harmonic form)   Arpeggios

2 f♯ minor (melodic form)   Arpeggios

Etude In F♯ Minor

3 Allegretto *mf* ... *mp* *cresc.* ... *f*

Liebestraum
(Excerpt)

FRANZ LISZT

4 A TONE STUDY — Listen carefully.
Slowly
mp ... *mf* ... *mp*

Etude

5 Allegro moderato
mf ... *f* ... *p* ... *p* ... *f*

INTERVALS

Articulation Study

Etude

SCHANTL

La Donna E Mobile

VERDI

28

Lip Slurs

2nd + 3rd Valves _____ 1st + 3rd Valves _____

Scale Study In A♭

Chromatic Scale

Also, tongue every note.

Etude

Maestoso

f marcato (with emphasis - marked)

piu mosso (more motion - quicker)

f minor (harmonic form) · Arpeggios

f minor (melodic form) · Arpeggios

Spanish Dance

Moderato · *mf*

Apply this pattern to various scales in different registers. Tongue cleanly.

Articulation Etude

SCHANTL

Agitato

Theme From "Poet And Peasant Overture"

von SUPPE

Slowly

INTERVALS

Triplet Etude

Moderato

Chromatic Etude

Czardas

HUNGARIAN DANCE

Allegro vivace

E Major Scale   Arpeggios

1

Scale Study In E Major

Work for speed!

2

INTERVAL STUDY
Slowly

3

F Minor Etude

Andantino

4

mf

Washington Post March

JOHN PHILIP SOUSA

March tempo

5

mf

1 c# minor (harmonic form) — Arpeggios

2 c# minor (melodic form) — Arpeggios

Etude In E Major

3 Allegro ma non troppo — staccato

Scale Study In F Minor

4

INTERVAL STUDY
5 Slowly

Nocturne
A. BORODIN

6 Moderato

*See page 39.

Db Major Scale   Arpeggios

INTERVALS

Scale Study In Db Major

Pastorale

SCHANTL

Andantino

Triple Tonguing

The performing of fast triplet passages requires a technique known as *triple tonguing*. This is achieved by the use of the syllables *Tu-Tu-Ku* repeated in rapid succession. However, before applying them to the horn practice them verbally.

Tu Tu Ku Tu Tu Ku Tu Tu Ku Tu Tu Ku   Tu

Apply triple tonguing to the following exercise. Start slowly and gradually increase your speed.

ARBAN

Tu Tu Ku Tu Tu Ku Tu   Tu Tu Ku Tu Tu Ku Tu   etc.

LIP SLURS

Apply to complete pattern (a)

2nd Valve _____ 1st Valve _____ 1st + 2nd Valves _____

Articulation Etude

Watch!

Rhythm Etude *

Moderato

*In playing modern contemporary music you will find many abrupt time changes. In this Etude the beat remains the same throughout.

Triple Tonguing

ARBAN

Work slowly and work for speed!

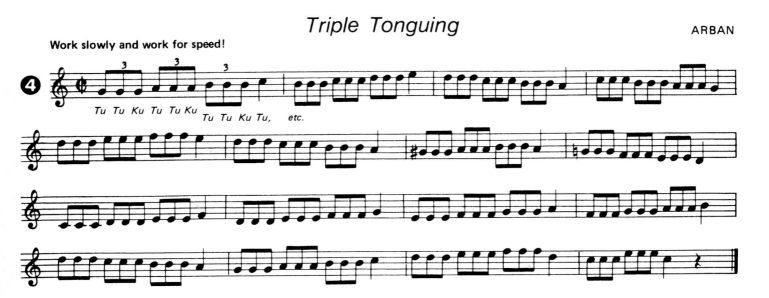

Tu Tu Ku Tu Tu Ku Tu Tu Ku Tu, etc.

Interval Study

Work for speed!

Chromatic Scale

Also play:

Andante

BEETHOVEN

Double Tonguing

The performing of fast duplet passages requires a technique known as *double tonguing*. This is achieved by the use of the syllables Tu - Ku repeated in rapid succession. Before applying them to the horn practice them verbally.

Tu Ku Tu Ku Tu Ku Tu Ku Tu

Apply double tonguing to the following exercise. Start slowly and gradually increase your speed.

ARBAN

Tu Ku Tu Ku Tu   Tu Ku Tu Ku Tu,   etc.

Additional Triple Tonguing and Double Tonguing exercises may be found in the supplementary book STUDIES AND MELODIOUS ETUDES, Level III.

Basic Technic

Lip Slurs

Chromatic Scale

Articulations

Intervals

Basic Technic (cont'd)

TRANSPOSITION

TRANSPOSE FOR HORNS IN E♭ and C.

Theme From "Rosamunde"

SCHUBERT

Triple Tonguing

Double Tonguing

Musical Embellishments
Grace Notes

A *short* grace note is written as a small eighth note with a dash through its stem. The grace note *precedes* the beat and is played in a light, unaccented manner.

AS WRITTEN:

AS PLAYED:

The *short* grace note may appear as single, double, triple or quadruple notation. However, they should still be played ahead of the beat on which the principal note appears.

AS WRITTEN:

AS PLAYED:

The *long* grace note (appoggiatura) does not have a dash through its stem and is played *on* the beat. The long grace note is assigned half the time value of the principal note. However, if it precedes a dotted note the grace note would receive two-thirds the time value of the principal note.

AS WRITTEN:

AS PLAYED:

The Mordent

The *mordent* is a musical ornamentation consisting of the rapid alternation of the given note with the note immediately below it in the scale. The sign for the mordent is . The *inverted mordent* consists of the alternation of the given note and the note immediately above in the scale. The sign for the inverted mordent is ♫.

AS WRITTEN:

AS PLAYED:

The Trill

AS WRITTEN:

The *trill* is a musical ornamentation consisting of the rapid alternation of a given note and the next note above in the diatonic scale. The interval may be a whole step or a half step. If an accidental accompanies the trill sign it alters the upper tone.

Longer trills are closed by playing a note one scale step below the given note following by the given note.

AS WRITTEN:

For solo playing it is advisable to start the trill slowly and gradually increase the speed.

The Turn (Gruppetto)

The *turn* is a musical ornamentation consisting of four notes including (1) the scale tone above the given note, (2) the given note, (3) the scale tone below the given note, and, (4) the given note again. The turn is indicated by this sign ∾ . The turn is executed very rapidly near the end of the duration of the given note.

AS WRITTEN:

When a turn is to be executed after a dotted note the last note of the turn is given the same value as the dot (Ex. 1). If an accidental is placed under a turn it alters the lower note (Ex. 2). If an accidental is placed over a turn it alters the upper note (Ex. 3). If the turn is placed *directly* over the given note it is executed very rapidly starting on the tone above the given note (Ex. 4).

AS WRITTEN: